BASIC ENGLISH SERIES

Poetry 1

John L. Foster

Macmillan Education

The **Basic English Series** consists of:

Poetry 1, 2 and 3
Story 1, 2 and 3
Drama 1, 2 and 3
Language 1, 2 and 3

First published 1987

Published by
MACMILLAN EDUCATION LTD
Houndmills, Basingstoke, Hampshire RG21 2XS
and London
Companies and representatives
throughout the world

Designed by Linda Reed
Illustrated by David Farris, Douglas Hall, Peter Joyce, Paul Stubbs

Printed in Hong Kong

British Library Cataloguing in Publication Data
Poetry 1. — (Basic English series)
1. Children's poetry, English
I. Foster, John L. (John Louis)
II. Series
821'.008   PR1175.3
ISBN 0-333-41576-0

Contents

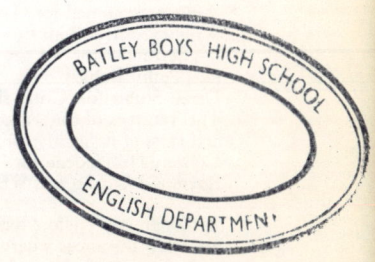

Acknowledgements

The author and publishers wish to thank the following who have kindly given permission for the use of copyright material:

Allison and Busby Ltd for 'What's That Down There?' by Adrian Mitchell from *Nothingmas Day*;

Angus and Robertson (UK) Ltd for 'Snake Glides' from *And I Dance* by Keith Bosley;

Arrow Publications for 'A Cello' by Richard Lester from *Poems For Fun* eds. Z and J. Woodward, Beaver Books and 'What would you like to be when you grow up, little girl?' by Jenny Craig from *The Beaver Book of School Verse* ed. J. Curry, Beaver Books;

Diane Brookens for 'Secret Wishes on a Bad Day';

Cambridge University Press for 'Have You Ever Seen?' by Grace Nichols and 'Richard's Brother Speaks' by Desmond Strachan from *I Like That Stuff* ed. Morag Styles;

Laura Cecil on behalf of the James Reeves Estate for 'Spells' from *James Reeves The Complete Poems*;

Stanley Cook for 'H' from *Alphabet*, Harry Chambers/Peterloo Poets and 'People' from *Concrete Poems*, The Keepsake Press;

Andre Deutsch Ltd for 'Mad Meals', 'Wise One' and 'I Know Someone' from *Quick Let's Get Out of Here* and 'Words in Space' from *Wouldn't you Like to Know?* by Michael Rosen, 'Here lies John Smith, exactly 8' and 'Here lies a family dog called Rover' from *Seen Grandpa Lately?* by Roy Fuller, and 'The Flower of Happiness' and four riddles from *Riddles, Rhymes and Rigmaroles* by John Cunliffe;

Gwen Dunn for 'Sewing Machine' from *Drumming in the Sky*, BBC Publications;

Eric Finney for 'Best Things, Worst Things' and a riddle;

The Folio Society for an Anglo Saxon riddle translated by Kevin Crossley-Holland from *The Exeter Riddle Book* (1978);

William Heinemann Ltd for 'What is White?' from *Hailstones and Halibut Bones* by Mary O'Neill, World's Work Ltd;

Geoffrey Holloway for 'Beat That';

Ian Larmont for 'The School Ghoul';

Elizabeth Lindsay for 'My Cat' from *Stories and Rhymes*, BBC Publications;

Macdonald & Co Ltd for 'Jamaica Market' by Agnes Maxwell-Hall from *Wheel Around The World* ed. Chris Searle;

Macmillan of Canada for 'Curse' from *Nicholas Knock and Other People* by Dennis Lee;

Wes Magee for 'An A-Z of Pop Groups';

Don Marquis for 'The Tom Cat' from Poems and Portraits by Don Marquis. Copyright 1917 by Sun Printing & Publishing Association, used by permission of Doubleday & Co. Inc.

John Mbiti for 'The Snake Song' from *My World — Poems from Living Language* ed. Joan Griffiths, BBC Publications;

North-west Arts for 'Grandfather' by Susan Hrynkow from *Young People's Poetry*;

Gareth Owen for 'Excuses, Excuses';

Punch for 'Noise' by Jessie Pope;

Alastair Reid for 'Words To Be Said on the Move', 'Odd Words', 'Light Words' and 'Heavy Words' from *Ounce, Dice, Trice*, J.M. Dent;

Rony Robinson for 'Alf Abets';

Robson Books Ltd for 'All about me' from *Witches, Smile Please* by Shelagh McGee;

William Scammell for 'The Song of Tyrannosaurus Rex' from *Poems for 10 and Over* ed. Kit Wright, Kestrel Books;

Ian Serraillier for 'To get rid of the 'flu' and 'To find a lost season ticket' from *I'll tell you a tale*, Puffin Books;

Derek Stuart for 'Child skipping' and 'Why is it?';

The Trustees of the Tagore Estate for 'Vocation', *The Crescent Moon* from *Collected Poems and Plays of Rabindranath Tagore*, Macmillan;

Colleen Thibaudeau for 'Balloon';

Raymond Wilson for 'Why?'.

Although every effort has been made to trace original sources and copyright owners there are a few instances where this was not possible. The publishers will be pleased to rectify any such omission in future editions.

1: List Poems

In this unit, we look at some poems in which the writers have developed their ideas in the form of a list. Three different types of list are presented. In the first two poems, *Best Things* and *Worst Things*, Eric Finney uses lists in order to express a young person's thoughts and feelings, in this case about his/her likes and dislikes. In her poem *Jamaica Market* Agnes Maxwell-Hall uses a list to describe a scene. Finally, Michael Rosen makes a list in order to present some odd and amusing ideas in his poem *Mad Meals*.

Best Things

Coke from the fridge,
Bananas, cherries,
Mum when she's had
A couple of sherries;
Ice cream and jelly,
Nearly everything on telly:
Cartoons, westerns,
Comedy, pop –
Start on that
I'll never stop;
The taste of parsley,
Vinegar, mustard,
School chocolate pudding
With green custard;

Waking up
On a Saturday morning:
Weekend thoughts dawning;
Old jeans –
Who cares if I get a rip in?
The taste of a Cox's Orange Pippin;
Sailing in a boat;
The smell of creosote;
Chips all squashy
From the shop in town,
Or Mum's chips, crisp
And golden brown;
Great blobs of candy floss
And hotdogs at the fair,
My bed, my new bike,
My favourite chair . . .

I could go on forever
If I wanted to –

And so, I expect, could you.

ERIC FINNEY

Worst Things

Boring grown-up talk on telly,
Putting my foot in an ice-cold welly;
The day I found my gerbil dead;
Getting out of bed;
Shopping with Mum for socks and vests,
Reading and writing tests;
Eggs boiled either too hard or too soft,
The spiders in our loft;
Mum and Dad quarrelling –

They'll make it up, I know;
Being kissed by my Auntie Flo;
Washing, cleaning shoes,
Hearing my sister humming;
Having the house all tidy and spotless
'Cos visitors are coming;
Big skinny dogs, new shoes and slippers,
Posh voices, smelly feet, kippers,
Parsnips, cabbage; losing things down grids;
Having different clothes
From all the other kids.

Stopping there for now:
Don't want to be a bore.
I might come back in half an hour
And think of fifty more.

ERIC FINNEY

Talking and writing

1 In pairs, talk about the things which the person in the two poems (a) likes, (b) dislikes.

Do you share any of the person's likes and dislikes?

Do you dislike anything which the person likes? Or like anything which the person dislikes?

2 Divide a piece of paper into two columns. Make lists of 'Things I like' and 'Things I hate'.

Tell your partner what makes you like and hate the things on your lists, then write a list poem about either 'Things I like' or 'Things I hate'.

3 Think about some times in your life that have been 'Best moments' and some that have been 'Worst moments'. Tell your partner about them and why they were the best or the worst moments. Write a poem about either 'Best moments' or 'Worst moments'.

4 Talk about things that frighten you or things that make you nervous.

Write a list poem about either 'Things that frighten me' or 'Things that make me nervous'.

Jamaica Market

Honey, pepper, leaf-green limes,
Pagan fruit whose names are rhymes,
Mangoes, breadfruit, ginger-roots,
Granadillas, bamboo-shoots,
Cho-cho, ackees, tangerines,
Lemons, purple Congo-beans,
Sugar, okras, kola-nuts,
Citrons, hairy coconuts,
Fish, tobacco, native hats,
Gold bananas, woven mats,
Plantains, wild-thyme, pallid leeks,
Pigeons with their scarlet beaks,
Oranges and saffron yams,
Baskets, ruby guava jams,
Turtles, goat-skins, cinnamon,
Allspice, conch-shells, golden rum.
Black skins, babel – and the sun
That burns all colours into one.

AGNES MAXWELL-HALL

In pairs

1 Talk about how the poet tries to make the market seem an exciting place by listing the names of all the fruits and vegetables on sale there. What other items are being sold in the market?

2 Point out all the places in the poem where colours are mentioned. What is the effect of including so many references to colours?

3 Notice how *Jamaica Market* has a strong rhythm, the effect of which is to suggest that the market is a lively, busy place. The lines are arranged in rhyming pairs, each line consisting of seven syllables and having the same rhythm.

Prepare a reading of the poem in which you and your partner try to bring out its rhythm. Divide up the poem so that you take it in turns to read two lines each. The first person reads lines 1 and 2, the second person reads lines 3 and 4, then the first person reads lines 5 and 6 and so on.

4 Take it in turns to close your eyes. Imagine you are walking through a Jamaican market. Tell your partner about some of the things you see.

Writing

Write a list poem in which you try to describe one of the following scenes: a busy railway-station, a market or a fairground.

Before you begin, make lists of (i) the things you would see, (ii) the sounds you would hear, (iii) the smells there would be.

When you write your poem, do not necessarily include

everything you put on your lists. Try to develop your poem
so that it manages to convey the atmosphere of the scene in
the way that Agnes Maxwell-Hall manages to convey the
atmosphere of the market.

Mad Meals

Grilled cork
Matchbox on toast
glass soup
roasted clock
ping-pong ball and chips
acorn sandwich
fillet of calculator
trouser salad
grilled lamp-post
ice-cream (vanilla, soap or pepper)

MICHAEL ROSEN

Writing

Try it yourself:

1 Write a ridiculous recipe for a dish such as pyjama pie or
toothpaste cake.

2 Make a list of daft drinks.

3 Write a mad menu for Crazy Charlie's Café.

4 Imagine you are a witch or a mad magician planning a
visit to the Sorcerer's Supermarket. Write out your shopping-
list.

2: Colour Poems and Sound Poems

Colour Poems

In a book of poems called *Hailstones and Halibut Bones*, Mary O'Neill wrote a series of poems about different colours. She explored the colours through all the senses, not just the sense of sight. For example, 'Red is a shout', while 'the sound of green is a water-trickle.' Grey is 'the velvet-soft' of a pussy willow and 'the wetness of melting slush,' while:
    'Black is beauty
    In its deepest form.'
Here is what she wrote about white:

What is white?

White is a dove
And lily of the valley
And a puddle of milk
Spilled in an alley –
A ship's sail
A kite's tail
A wedding veil
Hailstones and
Halibut bones
And some people's
Telephones.

The hottest and most blinding light
Is white.
And breath is white
When you blow it out on a frosty night.
White is the shining absence of all colour
Then absence is white
Out of touch
Out of sight.
White is marshmallow
And vanilla ice cream
And the part you can't remember
In a dream.
White is the sound
Of a light foot walking
White is a pair of
Whispers talking.
White is the beautiful
Broken lace
Of snowflakes falling
On your face.
You can smell white
In a country room
Near the end of May
When the cherries bloom.

MARY O'NEILL

Talking and writing

Work in a group

1 List all the white objects that Mary O'Neill mentions in the poem. What other things that are white can you think of (e.g. a blank piece of paper)?

2 Talk about how Mary O'Neill uses the senses of (a) taste, (b) sound, in the poem. Which foods does she say are white? Can you think of any others? Which sounds does she say are white? Can you suggest other 'white' sounds?

3 How does she use the senses of (a) touch, (b) smell, in the poem?

4 Why does she say (a) 'absence is white'?, (b) 'white is... the part you can't remember in a dream'?

5 Take it in turns to say which lines in the poem you think are the most effective and why.

Work in pairs

Choose any colour. It could be one of the colours of the spectrum – violet, indigo, blue, green, yellow, orange and red – or any other colour, e.g. brown, gold, azure, pink, grey, bronze, silver, dun, fawn, mustard, vermillion, magenta, bay, turquoise, etc. Do a brainstorm and write down on a piece of paper all the objects, ideas, feelings and moods you associate with that colour.

Here is an example of the start of a brainstorm on the colour red:

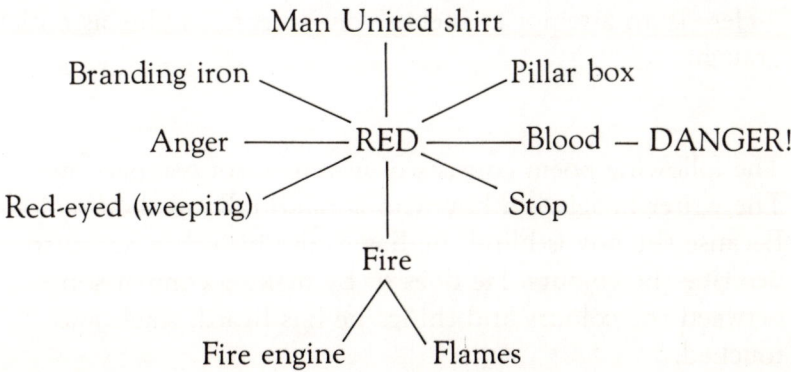

When you have finished, join up with a pair who chose a different colour. See if you can suggest any ideas to add to theirs and if they can suggest any ideas to add to yours.

Write a poem about a colour in the way that Mary O'Neill has written about white. As you write, think about the sounds which Mary O'Neill says are white. Which sound(s) fit your colour? Can you think of (a) a taste, (b) a touch, (c) a smell which fit your colour? Try in your poem to explore the colour using all your senses in the way that Mary O'Neill does in *What is white*?

COMPARISON POEMS

Sometimes, when we speak about colours, we use comparisons. For example, we say that someone looked as white as a sheet or as red as beetroot. Such expressions have been used so many times that they have lost much of their force. Any over-used expression, which has lost its force, is known as a cliche.

Think up comparisons for three or four different colours. Try to make an unusual connection of ideas and to avoid clichés.

Here is an attempt at such a comparison: as blue as an icy draught.

The following poem consists of a number of comparisons. The writer imagines a boy who is blind talking about colour. Because the boy is blind, he has to use his other senses to describe the colours. He does so by making comparisons between the colours and things he has heard, smelt and touched.

I Asked the Little Boy who Cannot See

I asked the little boy who cannot see,
'And what is colour like?'
'Why, green,' said he,
'Is like the rustle when the wind blows through
The forest; running water, that is blue;
And red is like a trumpet sound; and pink
Is like the smell of roses; and I think
That purple must be like a thunderstorm;
And yellow is like something soft and warm;
And white is a pleasant stillness when you lie
And dream.'

ANON.

Writing

Try it yourself. Write a poem which consists of comparisons
between colours and things you hear, smell, taste or touch.

Sound poems

Noise

I like noise.
The whoop of a boy, the thud of a hoof,
The rattle of rain on a galvanized roof,
The hubbub of traffic, the roar of a train,
The throb of machinery numbing the brain,
The switching of wires in an overhead tram,
The rush of the wind, a door on the slam,
The boom of the thunder, the crash of the waves,
The din of a river that races and raves,
The crack of a rifle, the clank of a pail,
The strident tattoo of a swift-slapping sail –
From any old sound that the silence destroys
Arises a gamut of soul-stirring joys.
I like noise.

JESSIE POPE

Talking and writing

1 Talk about the sounds Jessie Pope mentions. Do you agree with her? Do you particularly like or dislike any of the sounds she likes?

2 Draw two columns on a piece of paper and make lists of (a) Sounds I Like and (b) Sounds I Hate. When you have finished, compare your lists and explain to each other why you like or dislike certain sounds.

3 Write a poem about either 'Sounds I like' or 'Sounds I can't stand'. Here are the first two lines of such a poem:

Sounds I Can't Stand
I can't stand the skriek of new chalk on a blackboard,
Or the scrunch when the edges of two coins are rubbed
    together...

Note: It is sometimes hard to find exactly the right word to describe a sound. Don't be afraid to make up, or coin, your own word to fit the sound, just as the writer has in the line above by coining the word 'skriek'.

4 Write a comparison poem about sounds in which a girl who is deaf describes different sounds by saying what she thinks they are like, using her senses of sight, touch, taste and smell to draw comparisons. One possible opening:

I asked the young girl who cannot hear,
'And what is sound like?'
'Why a roar,' she said,
'Is like...

THE SOUNDS OF THE FAIR

Here is how the author Charles Dickens described the sounds of a nineteenth-century fair:

Imagine yourself in an extremely dense crowd, which swings you to and fro, and in and out, and every way but the right one; add to this the screams of women, the shouts of boys, the clanging of gongs, the firing of pistols, the ringing of bells, the bellowings of speaking-trumpets, the squeaking of penny dittoes, the noise of a dozen bands, with three drums in each, all playing different tunes at the same time, the hallooing of showmen, and an occasional roar from the wild-beast shows; and you are in the very centre and heart of the fair.

from *Sketches by Boz*

Talking and writing

1 Talk about the noises Dickens mentions and the words he chooses to describe the sounds. Some of the words he uses are particularly effective because they sound like and remind us of the noises themselves. Which words do you think achieve this best?

2 Suggest alternative words that Dickens could have used to describe each of the sounds. For example, he could have written 'the *shrieks* of women' instead of 'the *screams* of women'. Redraft the passage, replacing each sound word with an alternative word. Compare your different versions of the passage. Decide whose version works best.

3 Look at the picture of a modern fairground scene. Think of the sounds you hear at a modern fair and make a list of them. Choose the words to describe the sounds carefully and, if possible, select words which sound like and remind us of the noises themselves.

4 Write a poem called 'The sounds of the fair.'

Dickens mentions the 'hallooing' of showmen. Here are some rhymes made up of the cries or calls that fairground sellers used in the past to attract people to buy their goods.

Fair cries

Buttons, a farthing a pair,
Come, who will buy them of me?
They are round and sound and pretty
And fit for the girls of the city.
Come, who will buy them of me?
Buttons, a farthing a pair.

Hot baked wardens, hot!
Ripe speregas!
Harti chokes!
Cherrie ripe!
Delicate cowcumbers!
Round and sound, fivepenny a pound,
Duke cherries!
Fresh gathered peas, young hastings!
Strawberries, scarlet strawberry!
Two bundles, scarlet strawberry!
Two bundles a penny, primroses!
Sweet violets, a penny a bunch!

Talking and writing

The cries were often sung in a musical way, just as advertising jingles are often sung on television today. Think of the various different types of stalls at a modern fair and the way the stallholders try to attract you to buy goods, to go on a ride, to try your skill at such things as shooting or throwing darts, or to step inside a booth to have your fortune told or to see something amazing. Work with a partner and write down some of the cries you hear at a modern fair. Then, either make up a number of sellers' cries and jingles, or write a poem called 'Fairground cries'.

Writing

Spider poems
A spider poem is a poem that spins itself out very thinly down the page like a spider's thread. It is also called a spider poem because despite its frailty it can trap and fix in a poem all the fluttering sensations of one moment.

Arm stick
Clattering down
Whirling
The bright fruits turning
Singly stopped
Crash
Crash
Crash
Lucky
Or nothing?

Imagine you are standing in the middle of a fairground. Think of all the different sounds you can hear. Picture all the different sights, colours and smells around you. Now, focus your attention on one particular source of pleasure at the fair, a sideshow or a ride, for example. What are its most important features?

Jot down, in the order they occur to you, the details about it that you notice. Next, think of one or two powerfully descriptive words that you could use to describe each detail and note them down. Then, start to draft your poem as a spider poem, by using a fresh line for each observation or feeling.

Here is another spider poem by an eleven-year-old boy:

Hot Dog Seller

'Hot dogs,
Come 'n get 'em
Very 'ot.
Just off the stove
Only 40 pence
Come 'n get 'em.'
He stands shouting
Behind his stall
It is red and white
Very small,
And his stove silver
And large.
The sizzling from the stove
The shouting from the man
Who sells 'em hot.

3: Chain Poems

As the name suggests, in a chain poem each line is linked to the previous one, like the links in a chain.

Here is a traditional African chain-song:

If a jackal bothers you, show it a hyena,
If a hyena bothers you, show it a lion,
If a lion bothers you, show it an elephant,
If an elephant bothers you, show it a hunter,
If a hunter bothers you, show him a snake,
If a snake bothers you, show it a stick,
If a stick bothers you, show it a fire,
If a fire bothers you, show it a river,
If a river bothers you, show it the wind,
If the wind bothers you, show it God.

Talking and writing

1 This is a traditional chant, which is why the word 'bothers' is repeated in each line. Work in pairs and suggest words which you could put instead of 'bothers' in each line. For example, in line six you could put either 'hisses at' or 'bites' or 'strikes at'.

When you have chosen words to put on each line instead of 'bothers', write out your new version of the poem. Then, compare your version with other people's versions and decide on a class version of the poem.

2 Write your own chain poem, giving advice on what to do if certain things bother you. Either make up your own first line or begin your first line like this: 'If a dog snarls at you...'.

3 Write a chain poem in which you suggest what to do if certain people bother you in any way. Either make up your own first line, or use this as your first line: 'If a teacher... you, send for...'.

The list of people you could include is endless, but here are some suggestions: your mother, father, brother, sister, aunt, uncle, granny, etc.; landlord, judge, doctor, dentist, fireman, policewoman, traffic warden, ghoul, witch, giant, vampire, wizard, executioner.

Here are two more chain poems:

The Key of the Kingdom

This is the Key of the Kingdom:
In that Kingdom there is a city;
In that city is a town;
In that town there is a street;
In that street there winds a lane;
In that lane there is a yard;
In that yard there is a house;
In that house there waits a room;
In that room an empty bed;
And on that bed a basket—
A basket of sweet flowers:
  Of flowers, of flowers;
  A basket of sweet flowers.

Flowers in a basket;
Basket on the bed;
Bed in the chamber;
Chamber in the house;
House in the weedy yard;
Yard in the winding lane;
Lane in the broad street;
Street in the high town;
Town in the city;
City in the Kingdom—
This is the Key of the Kingdom,
Of the Kingdom this is the Key.

ANON.

The Flower of Happiness

This is the flower of happiness,
That grows in a meadow,
That is in a valley,
That is in a land,
That is by a sea,
That is in an ocean,
That is in a world,
That is in a dream,
Dreamed by a girl,
Who is in a bed;
The bed is in a room,
The room is in a house,
The house is in a street,
The street is in a town,
The town is in a land,

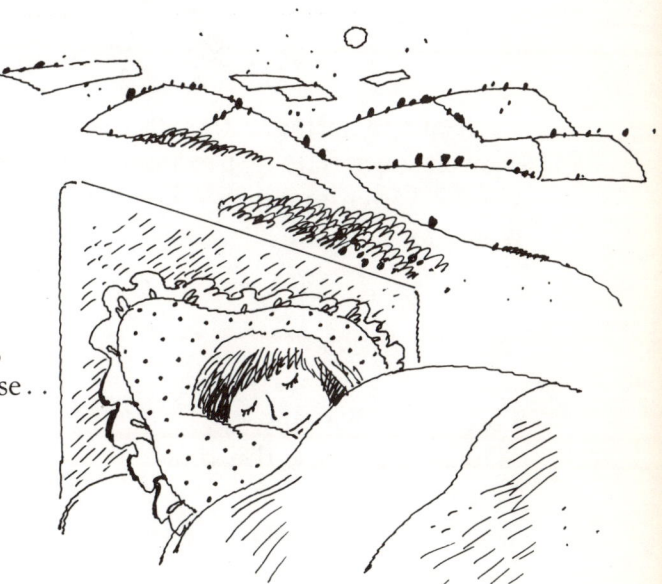

The land is by a sea,
The sea is in an ocean,
The ocean is in a world,
Wherein the flower of happiness grows,
In a meadow,
That is in a valley,
That is in a land,
That is by a sea,
That is in an ocean,
That is in a world,
That is in a dream,
Dreamed by a girl,
Who is in a bed;
The bed is in a room,
The room is in a house...

JOHN CUNLIFFE

Writing

Try it yourself:

1 Write a chain poem which begins:
    'This is the note
    That was found...'
  or 'On the hill there stands a castle...'.

2 Write a chain poem about one of the following:
    The pearl of wisdom
    The feather of truth
    The fountain of hope
    The snowflake of peace

4: Conversation Poems

Each of the poems in this unit consists of part of a conversation. The first example is an extract from a poem by Gareth Owen in which a boy explains to his teacher why he is late for school.

'Excuses, Excuses!'

Late again Blenkinsopp?
What's the excuse this time?
Not my fault sir.
Who's fault is it then?
Grandma's sir.
Grandma's? What did she do?
She died sir.
Died?
She's seriously dead alright sir.
That makes four grandmothers this term Blenkinsopp
And all on P. E. days.
I know. It's very upsetting sir.
How many grandmothers have you got Blenkinsopp?
Grandmothers sir? None sir.
You said you had four.
All dead sir.
And what about yesterday Blenkinsopp?
What about yesterday sir?

You were absent yesterday.
That was the dentist sir.
The dentist died?
No sir. My teeth sir.
You missed the maths test Blenkinsopp!
I'd been looking forward to it sir.
Right, line up for P.E.
Can't sir.
No such word as 'can't' Blenkinsopp.
No kit sir.
Where is it?
Home sir.
What's it doing at home?
Not ironed sir.
Couldn't you iron it?
Can't sir.
Why not?
Bad hand sir.
Who usually does it?
Grandma sir.
Why couldn't she do it?
Dead sir.

GARETH OWEN

Talking and writing

1 Although Gareth Owen does not use speech marks in the poem, it is easy enough to follow who is speaking in the poem, because of the way he always starts a new line for a new speaker. With a partner, read the poem aloud, one of you being the teacher and the other Blenkinsopp.

2 With your partner, think about situations in which you make up excuses. Make lists of the excuses you could use in such situations. Don't be afraid to make your excuses as far-fetched as Blenkinsopp's are. Here are some situations to think up excuses for:

To explain why you have forgotten to do your homework.
To explain how you happened to break a window.
To explain how you came to rip your jeans.
To explain why you did badly in a test.
To explain why you were somewhere that is out of bounds.
To explain where you have been when you have arrived home late.
To explain why you haven't had time to tidy your room.

3 Choose one of the situations you have discussed and one of the excuses from your list. Act out a scene in which an adult questions a girl or boy, and a conversation takes place in which the girl or boy develops the excuse, just as Blenkinsopp develops his excuse in Gareth Owen's poem.

4 Write your own conversation poem called *The Excuse*. Either make up your own beginning, or start with a question such as: 'Where's your homework?' or 'Where've you been? You're two hours late.'

If you decide not to use speech marks in your poem, make sure you make it clear where the speaker changes by lining your poem carefully and starting a new line whenever a new speaker speaks.

In the next poem, Michael Rosen imagines a group of children boasting to each other about the things they can do.

I Know Someone

I know someone who can
take a mouthful of custard and blow it
down their nose.
I know someone who can
make their ears wiggle.
I know someone who can
shake their cheeks so it sounds
like ducks quacking.
I know someone who can
throw peanuts in the air and catch them
in their mouth.
I know someone who can
balance a pile of 12 2p pieces on his elbow
and snatch his elbow from under them
and catch them.
I know someone who can
bend her thumb back to touch her wrist.
I know someone who can
crack his nose.
I know someone who can
say the alphabet backwards.
I know someone who can put their hands in
their armpits and blow raspberries.
I know someone who can
wiggle her little toe.
I know someone who can
lick the bottom of her chin.
I know someone who can
slide their top lip one way
and their bottom lip the other way,
and that someone is
ME.

MICHAEL ROSEN

Writing

1 Make up your own 'I know someone' poem, like Michael Rosen's, which consists of children boasting about things they can do.

2 Write an 'I know someone' poem in which children make ridiculous boasts about people in order to try to outdo each other. Here is an example of the beginning of such a poem:

I know someone who swam
across the Atlantic backstroke
twice in under twenty-four hours...

3 Write an 'I know someone' poem about yourself. Think of the most unusual and interesting things that have happened to you. Perhaps you have been to lots of schools or had an unusual pet. Or perhaps you once fell downstairs or had an accident of some kind. Or maybe you left the bathroom tap on and flooded the whole house. If you cannot think of enough true things to include in your poem, make some things up.

Here is another conversation poem in which children are trying to outdo each other:

Beat That

Saturday a wasp arrived. In
Man United colours. Beat that, he says.
It stopped on the telly till we'd won.
Wasps don't follow football?
This one did, he says.

Sunday our Steve ate a worm.
It crawled out of his nose. Beat that, I say.
Then we lost it in a plate of spaghetti.
Worms don't go for Italian food?
This one did, I say.

Yesterday we'd a death watch beetle
in the spin drier. Beat that, he says.
It flew out and ticked on the formica.
They don't fly – or tick in daytime?
This one did, he says.

Last night our gerbil got out.
It bit through the wiring. Beat that, I say.
We ran out of matches chasing candles.
Through the wiring? Their teeth aren't that strong.
This one's were, I say.

Tomorrow we've got an elephant coming
to empty our dustbin. Beat that, he says.
He'll curl his trunk round, and smack, it's in.
They're too big, can't get down the path?
This one will, he says.

Tomorrow our back loo tarantula's
dropping round for tea. Beat that, I say.
It's looped round the chain and flushed it twice.
Tarantulas don't go in back loos?
This one does, I say.

GEOFFREY HOLLOWAY

Writing

1 Notice how each verse in Geoffrey Holloway's poem follows the same pattern. In the first three lines one of the children claims that an animal did something amazing. In the fourth line, the other child questions whether that particular animal could do such a thing. Then, in the fifth line, the person who is making the claim states: 'This one did.' Work with a partner. Use the same verse pattern and write one or two verses to add to the poem.

2 Write a 'Beat that' conversation poem in which two children try to outdo each other making boasts about the things they saw on the way to school. Here is the start of such a poem:

On my way to school I saw a woman
with a rolling pin chasing a dinosaur
out of her vegetable patch.
Beat that, she says.
That's nothing, I say.
On my way to school I saw...

3 Write a conversation poem in which two children boast about the presents each one is going to get at Christmas or for her birthday. Develop the poem so that by the end of it the two children are making very far-fetched, ridiculous boasts.

Richard's Brother Speaks

Richard...
What's the matter? Why you not smiln' no more?
You wretch, you bruk the window?
Daddy a go peel you 'kin,
'Im a go peel it like how he peel orange.
When Daddy come true dat door.
You better run.
You better leave de country!
'Im a-go peel you 'kin.
You bottom a go warm tonight though!
Me goin' cook dinner pon you backside
When 'im done wid you
Richard 'im a come!
Run, bwoy, run!

DESMOND STRACHAN

Writing

1 'I wouldn't like to be you, when they find out.' Write a poem in which a girl or boy speaks to a sister or a brother who, like Richard, is going to be in big trouble when Mum or Dad finds out what has been going on.

2 'Don't you dare do that again – or else!' Write a poem in which an older girl or boy threatens a younger sister or brother, listing all the things that will happen 'if you dare do that again.'

3 Write a poem in which a mum or a dad speaks, telling a child off for something the child has done wrong.

5: Acrostics and Wordplays

A poem in which the first letters of the first word in each line together form a word is known as an acrostic. Here are some acrostics written by pupils in which the word 'school' is formed.

School is
Codswallop
Holidays are
Obviously ace
Oh no, back to school, dreadful!
Lessons again!

DAVID NUTTALL

School, who wants to go to school?
Classes for almost five hours a day,
How boring!
Or even more, if you get a detention.
Oh, why don't the teachers go home?
Lord help me!

MATTHEW WILLIAMS

School is O. K. I think!
Computers bleeping their buttons off,
Help!
Obey everything teachers say
Or else!
Look, think and listen!

KELVIN SIBLEY

Writing

Try it yourself.

1 Write an acrostic in which one of these words is formed:
Teacher, Lessons, Homework, Detention, Exams, Reports,
Excuses, Holidays.

2 Write an acrostic in which your name is formed. Here is
an example:

Just ace.
Out of this world.
Handsome, Heroic, Honest, Hard-working.
Number One!

Words in Space

They decided to abolish the words:
to sit
to stand
and to lie
and the word
to float will replace them.

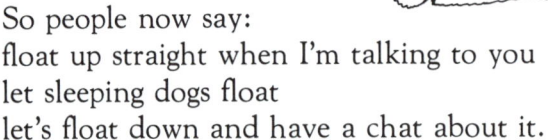

So people now say:
float up straight when I'm talking to you
let sleeping dogs float
let's float down and have a chat about it.

People who don't like cabbage say,
I can't float cabbage
and they watch telly
in the floating-room.

Is there anyone who doesn't
underfloat what I'm saying?

MICHAEL ROSEN

Writing

Try it yourself:

1 Write a similar poem about a situation in which a decision
has been taken to abolish *either* the words to speak, to talk
and to say and to replace them with the word to bleat *or* the
words to laugh, to smile and to grin and to replace them
with the word to gargle.

2 Imagine you have been chosen as the Minister for Language Development and it is your job to introduce a new law banning the use of unpleasant words. Make a list of words you do not like for any reason, perhaps simply because you do not like their sound or perhaps because you think they have unpleasant associations. Beside each word write down another word – the word you have chosen to replace the word that is to be banned.

When you have drawn up your list, compare it with other people's lists. Then write a poem called *The Language Law* announcing the changes and saying what will happen to anyone who disobeys the law.

Words

Words To Be Said on the Move	Odd Words *(to be spoken out loud, for fun)*
FLIT	HOBNOB
FLUCTUATE	BARLEY
WOBBLE	DOG-EARED
WIGGLE	HOPSCOTCH
SHIVER	WINDWARD
TIPTOE	OAF
PIROUETTE	EGG
TWIRL	OBOE
TEETER	NUTMEG
	OBLONG

ALASTAIR REID

Light Words *(to be said in windy or singing moods)*	Heavy Words *(to be used in gloom or bad weather)*
ARIEL	DUFFLE
WILLOW	BLUNDERBUSS
SPINNAKER	GALOSHES
WHIRR	BOWL
LISSOM	BEFUDDLED
SIBILANT	MUGWUMP
PETTICOAT	PUMPKIN
NIMBLE	CRUMB
NIB	BLOB

ALASTAIR REID

Writing

Try it yourself. Make your own lists of words:

1 Soft words.
2 Sharp words.
3 Strong words and weak words.
4 Mean words and generous words.
5 Bossy words (to be barked as orders).
6 Timid words (to be whispered quietly in corners).
7 Vicious words (to be snarled).
8 Polite words (to be spoken when answering the telephone).

6: Concrete Poems and Shaped Poems

Concrete Poems

A concrete poem is a poem in which words are presented in a pictorial way. The simplest type of concrete poem is one in which the letters of a single word are positioned so that the pictorial effect reflects the word's meaning, as in Derek Stuart's poem *Child Skipping* (overleaf).

In other single-word concrete poems, the letters of the word are drawn, so that the picture of the word illustrates its meaning. Stanley Cook's poem *People* is an example of such a poem.

STANLEY COOK

Child Skipping

```
        k i
    s        p
        k i
    s        p
        k i
    s        p
        k i
    s        p
        k i
    s        p
        k i
    s        p
        k i
    s        p
        k i
    s        p
        k i
```
                                         DEREK STUART

Talking and writing

1 In pairs, talk about Stanley Cook's poem. How does the picture of the word suggest its meaning?

2 Stanley Cook has written that 'there is a core of words in our language...that have the right look for their meaning.' Draw up a list of six words which you think have the right look for their meaning. Then, discuss your list with a partner and explain why you think those words do look right.

3 Choose a word which you think has the right look for its meaning and design your own concrete poem.

Shaped Poems

A shaped poem is one in which the words or the lines of the poem are arranged to form a particular shape. In the simplest type of shaped poem, the words of the poem form the shape of an object, as in Colleen Thibaudeau's *Balloon* and Richard Lester's *A cello*. In other shaped poems, the length of the line and how the lines are positioned on the page are used to create a visual effect which reinforces the poem's meaning. This is the technique used by Keith Bosley in his poem *Snake Glides*.

Balloon

```
            as
         big   as
      ball as round
     as sun . . . I tug
    and pull you when
    you run and when
      wind blows I
       say polite
           ly
            H
            O
            L
            D
            M
            E
             T
              I
              G
               H
                T
                L
                 Y.
```

COLLEEN THIBAUDEAU

A Cello

My cello big and fat

makes
the sound
of a screeching
rat. It plays F
double   sharp
when I want
it to play
B flat. It
sounds   like
a   bad   com-
position   when
I   play   in   the   4th
position.   If   I   try
to   play   vibrato   my
bow   goes   all
s - t - a - c - c -
ato
!

RICHARD LESTER

Writing

A shaped poem can be about any kind of object, such as a kettle or a kite, a dagger or a diamond, a frying pan or a flute.

Choose an object and draw its outline in pencil, then start trying to fit the words of a poem into the outline.

Points to consider as you write:

1 Colleen Thibaudeau's and Richard Lester's poems both rhyme, but a shaped poem does not have to rhyme. It is far more important that you choose words and phrases which accurately describe the object's features rather than that you should make the poem rhyme.

2 At the start of *Balloon*, Colleen Thibaudeau uses two simple comparisons to describe the balloon's size and shape. Similarly, Richard Lester's first sentence contains two adjectives describing the cello's size and shape. In your poem, use either adjectives and/or comparisons to describe the size and shape of the object.

3 In both *Balloon* and *A cello* the writers suggest that the objects behave as if they are alive. In *Balloon*, Colleen Thibaudeau does this by presenting the words of the poem as if the balloon is speaking them. Because the balloon is behaving as if it is a person, we say that the balloon is personified. When a writer presents an object or an animal in a poem as if it were a person, we say that he or she is using a technique known as personification.

   In *A cello*, Richard Lester hints that the cello has a will of its own when he suggests, in the second sentence, that his failure to produce the right note is the instrument's fault.

   As you draft your poem, consider whether or not you want to suggest that your object has a will of its own, as Richard Lester does, or to personify it as Colleen Thibaudeau does.

4 Notice how the exclamation mark is used at the end of Richard Lester's poem as part of the shape of the cello. Could a punctuation mark or, perhaps, a capital letter be used in a similar way in your poem?

Snake Glides

Snake glides
   through grass
     over
       pebbles
         forked tongue
      working
    never
  speaking
     but its
      body
       whispers
        listen   KEITH BOSLEY

Talking and writing

1 Talk about how the line-breaks of the poem suggest the way the snake moves.

2 Discuss Keith Bosley's choice of words by considering some alternatives that he could have used.
(a) Why do you think he chose 'glides' rather than, say, 'weaves', 'slithers' or 'slips'?
(b) Why do you think he chose 'through grass' rather than 'between the grass blades'?
(c) Why does he say the forked tongue is 'working' rather than 'darting'?
(d) Why does he say its body 'whispers' rather than 'mutters'?

3 Try it yourself. Write a poem about an animal moving, in which you use the line-breaks to reinforce the idea behind your poem. Choose your own title or use one of the following: *Salmon Leaps, Lion Prowls, Kangaroo Bounds, Cat Crawls.*

7: Portrait Poems

Each of the poems in this unit presents a picture or portrait.
In the first poem, Elizabeth Lindsay is more concerned to
portray her cat's mischievous character and her feelings
about her cat than to describe its physical appearance. So
she writes about what her cat has done rather than giving
details of what it looks like.

My Cat

My cat
Stole the meat from the window sill
My mum's so mad that she could kill.

My cat
Pounced on the leaves the sudden wind blew
And she flattened Dad's marigolds as she flew.

My cat
Sneaked through our neighbour's open back door
And pulled all her sausages onto the floor.

My cat
Hooked a fish from Mr Jones's tank
If she gets caught he'll give her a spank.

My cat
Helped our Dad when he painted the door
He left white paint footprints all over the floor.

My cat
Gave us a nice surprise
Not just one kitten but three four five.

My cat
Does nothing right or wrong
She's eighteen years old and sleeps all day long.

ELIZABETH LINDSAY

Talking and writing

Talk about your pets and how they behave. Tell the rest of
the class about any things you have trained them to do and
about any mischief they get up to. Recall any escapades in
which they have been involved, perhaps when they escaped,
got trapped, lost or injured.

Write a poem about your pet in the way that Elizabeth
Lindsay has written about her cat, concentrating more on
describing its character and what it does rather than what it
looks like.

Note: If you do not have a pet of your own, you could write
a poem called *Next-door's Dog* or *Next-door's Cat*.

Here is another poem about an animal. In this poem, Don
Marquis describes the tomcat's features as well as how it
behaves.

The Tomcat

At midnight in the alley
A tomcat comes to wail,
And he chants the hate of a million years
As he swings his snaky tail.

Malevolent, bony, brindled,
Tiger and devil and bard,
His eyes are coals from the middle of hell
And his heart is black and hard.

He twists and crouches and capers
And bares his curved sharp claws,
And he sings to the stars of the jungle nights
Ere cities were or laws.

Beast from a world primeval,
He and his leaping clan,
When the blotched red moon leers over the roofs,
Give voice to their scorn of man.

He will lie on a rug tomorrow
And lick his silk fur,
And veil the brute in his yellow eyes,
And play he's tame, and purr.

But at midnight in the alley
He will crouch again and wail,
And beat the time for his demon's song
With the swing of his demon's tail.

DON MARQUIS

Talking

1 What impression does the poem give you of the tomcat? What words would you use to describe his nature?

2 To what does Don Marquis compare the tomcat in the poem? How does this help him to achieve his aim?

3 Look carefully at the fifth verse. What does it tell us about the animal? How does this verse help to stress the impression of the tomcat Don Marquis is trying to create in the rest of the poem?

4 Don Marquis helps to build up the impression he is trying to create by the choice of words he uses to describe the various features and characteristics of the tomcat. Find the words he uses to bring to life the features listed below, and discuss why they are so effective:
(a) its song; (b) its tail; (c) its body; (d) its eyes; (e) its heart; (f) its movements; (g) its claws.

Writing

Choose an animal and write a poem about it so as to stress what you consider to be the characteristics that make it something to be loved or feared, to be treated with sympathy or to be scorned. Describe its features with care so as to build up the impression of it that you wish to create.

  Before drafting your poem, look at the questions below. They are all concerned with the various features of animals. Think of the words you would use to describe these features of your particular animal, and also of comparisons to express outstanding characteristics which it may have. When you have completed your list of words and comparisons, start to draft your poem. Do not necessarily include all the words and comparisons from your list in the poem, but only those which suit your purpose and help to build up the most vivid impression of your animal.

1 How would you describe its head? Its ears? Its eyes? Its nose? Its mouth? Its teeth? What are they like?
2 How would you describe its body? Its legs? Its arms? Its claws? Its tail? What are they like?
3 How would you describe its hair? Its skin? What would it feel like if you were to touch it?
4 How does it move? What does it move like?
5 How would you describe the noises it makes? What are they like?

All About Me

My hat is tall and pointed,
My nose is long and thin;
My thumbs are double-jointed,
For I drink a lot of gin.
My hair is long and greasy,
My clothes are not too smart –
Don't smirk – it would be easy
To make you fall apart!
I'm clever and I'm cunning,
I'm speedy, swift and fleet,
I'm very good at running
Because I've two left feet.
I'm always gay and carefree,
I love the life I live,

I drink a lot of herb-tea,
I make it in a sieve.
And when I feel like dancing,
Green monsters I invite,
But we never start our prancing
Till twelve o'clock at night!

SHELAGH MCGEE

Talking and writing

1 What impression is Shelagh McGee trying to get the witch to give of herself in the poem? Talk about how she builds up this impression by getting the witch to give details of (a) her appearance, (b) what she can do, (c) what the witch considers to be the main features of her character.

2 Build up a portrait poem about a witch in the way that you built up a portrait poem about an animal. Before you begin to draft your poem, list all the witch's features and jot down words and comparisons which you could use to describe them.

3 Write an 'All about me' poem in which another person, such as an elf or a giant, a goblin or an orc, a wizard or a spellcaster describes herself or himself in the way that the witch describes herself in Shelagh McGee's poem. Before you begin, decide what impression you want the person to give of herself or himself in the poem.

4 Write an 'All about me' poem about yourself. You could either make it a serious poem in which you try to give an honest impression of yourself or you could write a light-

hearted poem in which you make far-fetched boasts about
yourself in order to give the impression that you are
absolutely ace.

In this poem, Susan Hrynkow builds up a picture of her
grandfather by including details of his appearance and also of
the things she remembers him doing. As the poem develops,
we get a clear insight into her feelings for her grandfather
when he was alive, and on his death.

Grandfather

I remember
His sparse white hair and lean face...
Creased eyes that twinkled when he laughed
And the sea-worn skin
Patterned to a latticework of lines.
I remember
His blue-veined, calloused hands.
Long gnarled fingers
Stretching out towards the fire –
Three fingers missing –
Yet he was able to make model yachts
And weave baskets.
Each bronzed Autumn
He would gather berries.
Each breathing Spring
His hands were filled with flowers.

I remember
Worshipping his fisherman's yarns.

Watching his absorbed expression
As he solved the daily crossword
With the slim cigarette, hand rolled,
Placed between his lips.
I remember
The snowdrops.
The impersonal hospital bed.
The reek of antiseptic.

I remember, too,
The weeping child
And wilting daffodils
Laid upon his grave.

SUSAN HRYNKOW

Talking and writing

1 Talk about the details of her grandfather's appearance and
behaviour that Susan Hrynkow remembers and how her
careful choice of words enables the reader to picture him. Go
through the poem, picking out the key words and phrases
she uses, and talk about how they help the reader to picture
her grandfather. Here are the first few lines of the poem with
such words and phrases underlined. Talk about each one,
then go carefully through the rest of the poem, picking out
the key words and phrases and talking about each of them in
turn.

    I remember

    His <u>sparse</u> white hair and <u>lean</u> face...

<u>Creased</u> eyes that <u>twinkled</u> when he laughed
And the <u>sea-worn</u> skin
<u>Patterned</u> to a <u>latticework of lines</u>.

2 Pick out the lines in the poem which most helped you to
understand how deeply Susan feels about her grandfather.

3 Notice how Susan uses the phrase 'I remember' to join
together the information about her grandfather and her
feelings for him that she wants to put across in the poem.
Write your own 'I remember' poem about an elderly relative
or neighbour who has died, or about someone you used to
know, but no longer see either because you or they have
moved to another area or another school.

Before you start to draft your poem, note down the
memories you have (a) of the person's appearance, (b) of the
person's behaviour, (c) of particular incidents involving the
person that you might include in the poem. Then, decide
what impression of the person you want the poem to give.
Select from your list of memories the details that will help
you to give that impression. As you draft your poem, choose
each word and phrase as carefully as Susan Hrynkow has
done.

8: Question Poems

Each of the poems in this unit is developed from a question or a series of questions. The first two poems, Raymond Wilson's *Why should the world be usual?* and Grace Nichols's *Have you ever seen?* are light-hearted nonsense poems. Derek Stuart's *Why is it?* is a reflective poem in which a boy questions why his dad is good at some things, but not at others. Adrian Mitchell's *What's that down there?* is an imaginative poem which suggests what might be lurking 'in the chilly black maze of a cave.' The final poem, Michael Rosen's *Wise one*, is a humorous poem consisting of a series of questions and wisecrack answers.

Why?

Why should the world be usual?
  It surely isn't right!
I don't want to confuse you all,
    BUT
  Why shouldn't day be night?

Why shouldn't snow be hot and black?
  Why shouldn't pigs have wings?
Why shouldn't the front be at the back?
    AND
  Why shouldn't dustmen be kings?

Why shouldn't marmalade taste like meat?
  Why shouldn't grass be red?
Why must we always stand on our feet
    WHEN
  We can stand on our head?

Why shouldn't star-fish sing like thrushes?
  Why shouldn't elephants fly?
Why shouldn't pork-pies grow on bushes?
    AND
  Why shouldn't the sea be dry?

I *won't* let the world be usual!
  And if you disagree
I really shall confuse you all,
    'COS
  Why shouldn't you be me?

RAYMOND WILSON

Talking and writing

Work with a partner and produce another version of this
poem. Use Raymond Wilson's first and last verses, but write
your own versions of verses 2, 3 and 4. Here is a verse from
another version of the poem:
  Why shouldn't a pencil wear a wig?
  Why shouldn't stamps smoke cigars?
  Why shouldn't a spider dance a jig?
    AND
  Why shouldn't camels drive cars?

In this next poem, Grace Nichols asks whether you have ever seen some unusual animals or some animals doing strange things.

Have You Ever Seen?

Have you ever seen
a blue tadpole
Have you ever seen
a spoilt-brat toad

Have you ever seen
a walking fish
Have you ever seen
a grunting chick

Have you ever seen
a singing spider
Have you ever seen
a dancing tiger

Have you ever seen
a monkey swimming
Have you ever seen
a turtle grinning

Have you ever?

GRACE NICHOLS

Writing

1 Write some verses to add to Grace Nichols's poem about animals that look unusual or behave strangely.

2 Write your own 'Have you ever seen?' poem about odd objects or machines which behave in an unusual way. Here is a verse from such a poem:

Have you ever seen
a motor bike crying?
Have you ever seen
a lawn mower flying?

When you have finished drafting your poem, copy it out neatly and illustrate it.

Why is it?

Why is it
that when we go to the park
to fly my kite,
the string always gets tangled
in the trees
and the kite gets torn,
while other kids' kites
go soaring and swooping?

Why is it
that when we play cricket
on the beach,
my dad always drops catches
and is out first ball,
while other kids' dads

hit the ball
over the breakwater
out into the sea?

Why is it
that when my mum asks my dad
to put up a picture
on the wall,
he drills a hole
that's far too big
and gets plaster everywhere?

Why is it
that when my dad
tells my sister and me stories
in the dark,
I can almost see
the creatures
and feel their hot breath?

DEREK STUART

Talking and writing

1 Talk about what the boy thinks of his father.

What happens when his dad (a) takes him kite-flying, (b) plays cricket on the beach, (c) puts up a picture, (d) tells stories in the dark?

What impression do you get from the poem of the boy's attitude to his father? Do you think he admires his father? feels let down by his father? has mixed feelings towards his father? Give your reasons.

2 Think about a person you know well – a friend or a
relative, or yourself. Jot down on a piece of paper the things
the person is good at doing and the things the person is not
so good at doing. Then, write your own 'Why is it?' poem in
which you ask why the person is good at some things, but
not at others.

What's That Down There?

What's that down there?
What's that moving?
What's that moving down in the dark
   of this chilly black maze of a cave?

Is it Sarallo –
The scarlet snake with the seven
Silver heads
And fangs that snap like a murder trap?

What's that down there?
What's that moving?
What's that moving down in the dark
   of this chilly black maze of a cave?

Is it Farranaway –
That back-cracking brute
With a hundred horns
And hoofs that hit like horrible hammers?

What's that down there?
What's that moving?

What's that moving down in the dark
　of this chilly black maze of a cave?

Is it Thilissa –
That slippery wisp of
A whispering ghost of a
Girl who died
In the moistness of mist
Which lies like a shroud on
The underground lake
down in the dark in this chilly black maze of a cave?

ADRIAN MITCHELL

Talking and writing

1 Talk about how Adrian Mitchell's description of the cave makes it seem a sinister, frightening place. Discuss the ideas that are suggested to you by his choice of words in the phrase 'down in the dark of this chilly black maze of a cave.'

2 Talk about the description of Sarallo.
(a) What colour is Sarallo's body? What colour are Sarallo's heads? What do the colours of Sarallo's body and heads suggest to you about Sarallo?
(b) What is the movement of Sarallo's fangs compared to? What does this comparison tell you about Sarallo?
(c) Pick out the six words in the description of Sarallo that begin with the letter s. When a poet uses words beginning with the same letter or letters having the same sound, we say that the poet is using alliteration. Why do you think Adrian Mitchell uses words beginning with the letter s in this description?

3 Talk about the descriptions of Farranaway and Thilissa. What use does Adrian Mitchell make of (a) alliteration, (b) comparisons in these descriptions?

Which of the two descriptions do you think is the more effective? Why?

4 In groups of three produce an illustrated version of the poem, by each copying out the opening verse and one of the descriptions. Draw an illustration to go with each one and mount your versions on card to put on the wall.

5 In groups of three, prepare a reading of the poem. Decide for yourselves how you are going to present the poem. You could all three chant the opening verse together or you could say one line each. Or you could take it in turns to say the whole verse. When you have worked out how you are going to present the poem, practise your presentation before giving it to the rest of the class.

Writing

Write your own 'What's down there?' poem. Either make up your own opening verse or use this as your opening:

What's that down there?
What's that moving?
What's that moving down in the depths
in the murky gloom of the bottomless pit?

Make up names for the creatures you describe, just as Adrian Mitchell has.

Wise One

Wise one, wise one
how long is a piece of string?

Twice as long as half its length.

Wise one, wise one
how do you kill a snake?

Put its tail in its mouth
and it'll eat itself up.

Wise one, wise one
What's at the end of a cat's tail?

A cat.

Wise one, wise one
How can I get a chick out of a boiled egg?

Feed it to the chicken
so it can lay it again.

Wise one, wise one
Why do bricklayers put mortar on bricks?

To keep the bricks together
and to keep the bricks apart.

Wise one, wise one
My parrot talks too much.

Give it a good book to read.

MICHAEL ROSEN

Writing

1 Write your own 'Wise one' poems consisting of a series of questions and wisecrack answers.

2 Make a list of objects which have parts that have the same names as parts of the human body, e.g. a comb which has teeth.

Here is the first verse of a 'How is it?' question poem about such objects:

How is it that hair combs have teeth
But they cannot chatter or bite?

Use your list and write some more verses to add to this poem, each beginning 'How is it that...'

9: Prayers, Spells and Curses

Prayers

There are a great many poems in which poets look at things from the point of view of animals. In these two poems, Brenda Happell imagines the prayers of a kangaroo and a worm.

A Kangaroo's Prayer

  God
I am the kangaroo
I love this world, but I am unhappy.
I wish to be protected
From the tall man with the fierce gun
Who endangers my life,
And makes me scared to go out.
  Please help me great God
                Amen!

BRENDA HAPPELL

A Worm's Prayer

Oh Lord!
I am a small worm
People tread on me and cut me in half.
I only ask you one small thing,
Guide me safely to a hole.
A safe hole with fresh moist dirt
In which I can squirm,
And friends to be with friends to love.
This is all I want oh Lord
to be happy.

Amen!

BRENDA HAPPELL

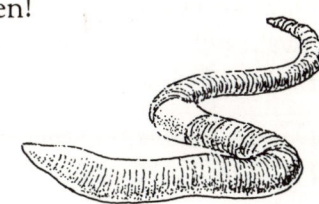

Talking and writing

1 Work in pairs.
(a) Talk about the sort of things pet animals might pray for.
What might the following pray for – a goldfish? a canary? a
hamster? a cat? a dog?
(b) Talk about the animals which are kept in circuses and
zoos. Suggest what they might pray for.
(c) Talk about some wild animals. How would their prayers
be different from those of animals kept as pets or kept in
captivity?

2 Write the prayers of three different animals – a pet animal,
a circus or zoo animal and a wild animal.

Spells

A spell is any series of words which are chanted or said in order to produce magical results. Often, a spell is a verse of some kind. Traditionally, spells are associated with witches and wizards. Here is the chant of the three witches as they make their spell in Shakespeare's *Macbeth*.

Round about the cauldron go:
In the poisoned entrails throw.
Toad, that under cold stone
Days and nights has thirty-one
Sweltered venom sleeping got,
Boil thou first in the charmed pot.

Double, double, toil and trouble;
Fire burn and cauldron bubble.

Fillet of a fenny snake,
In the cauldron boil and bake;
Eye of newt and toe of frog,
Wool of bat and tongue of dog,
Adder's fork and blind-worm's sting,
Lizard's leg and howlet's wing,
For a charm of powerful trouble,
Like a hell-broth boil and bubble.

Double, double, toil and trouble;
Fire burn and cauldron bubble.

WILLIAM SHAKESPEARE

In groups

In groups of three, work out a dramatic presentation of the witches' chant. Use music and sound effects and, if possible, lighting effects. Learn the chant and then present it to the rest of the class.

Writing

Write a poem called *Witches' Brew*. Make the ingredients of your brew as unpleasant as possible.

When we think of spells, we usually think of evil and of unpleasant results. But spells can be recited in order to charm away evil or to bring about pleasant results. Here are two spells which are designed to bring about pleasant results.

To get rid of the 'flu

First day – freeze and bake;
Second day – shiver and shake;
Third day – 'flu fly!
But if you sit in the snow you'll die.

IAN SERRAILLIER

To find a lost season ticket

Stay, if fallen on the floor;
Flap, if hidden behind a door;
Jump, if in some guilty pocket;
Hear me, hear me,
Season ticket!
If I sing the spell in vain,
I cannot come to school again.

IAN SERRAILLIER

Writing

Try it yourself:

1 Write a spell with one of the following aims:
To make the school be closed for a day.
To drive away toothache or stomach-ache.
To repair a window broken during a football game.
To frighten away the bogeyman.
To find a lost brooch.
To ensure a good school report.

2 Write a spell to do one of the following:
To calm the wind on a stormy night.
To drive away the blizzard and thaw the ice.
To bring rain to a parched land.

Here is another type of poem about spells:

Spells

I dance and dance without any feet –
This is the spell of the ripening wheat.

With never a tongue I've a tale to tell –
This is the meadow-grasses' spell.

I give you health without any fee –
This is the spell of the apple-tree.

I rhyme and riddle without any book –
This is the spell of the bubbling brook.

Without any legs I run for ever –
This is the spell of the mighty river.

I fall for ever and not at all –
This is the spell of the waterfall.

Without a voice I roar aloud –
This is the spell of the thunder-cloud.

No button or seam has my white coat –
This is the spell of the leaping goat.

I can cheat strangers with never a word –
This is the spell of the cuckoo-bird.

We have tongues in plenty but speak no names –
This is the spell of the fiery flames.

The creaking door has a spell to riddle –
I play a tune without any fiddle.

JAMES REEVES

Talking and writing

1 Why is the poem called *Spells*?

2 Each pair of lines in the poem is like a short riddle, followed by its answer. Which two lines in the poem do you think make the best riddle? Compare your choice with those of other members of your group.

3 Try it yourself. See if you can produce some spells like those in James Reeves' poem. Here is one attempt to do so:
    I cough, I splutter, I can't run very far –
    This is the spell of the broken-down car.

Curses

Curse

ON A DRIVER
WHO SPLASHED HIS NEW PANTS
WHEN HE COULD
HAVE JUST AS EASILY
DRIVEN
AROUND THE PUDDLE

May your large intestine freeze in a knot like a skate-lace!
May manhole covers collapse wherever you go.
May garbage strikes pester your street, and may you
grow eight new
Feet and get poison ivy on every toe!

DENNIS LEE

Writing

Try it yourself. Write a curse. Either make up your own title
or write a curse on one of the following:

ON A TEACHER
WHO KEPT US IN AT FOUR O'CLOCK
FOR NOT DOING OUR HOMEWORK
WHEN HE COULD JUST AS EASILY
HAVE WAITED
FOR US TO HAND IT IN TOMORROW.

ON A FRIEND
WHO SAID SHE'D COME ROUND
AT HALF-PAST SIX
BUT DIDN'T TURN UP
BECAUSE SHE COULDN'T BE BOTHERED,
BECAUSE SHE SAID THERE WAS
A GOOD PROGRAMME ON TV.

ON WHOEVER IS IN CHARGE
OF THE WEATHER
AND SENT A THUNDERSTORM
WHILE I WAS WAITING FOR THE BUS
WHEN HE COULD JUST AS EASILY
HAVE WAITED
UNTIL I WAS INDOORS

Here is another curse. In this curse, the speaker is cursing a
place rather than another person. His victim is an Australian
town called Tallarook.

McQuade's Curse

May Satan, with a rusty crook,
Catch every goat in Tallarook;
May Mrs Melton's latest spook
Haunt all old maids in Tallarook;
May China's oldest pig-tailed cook
Spoil chops and steaks in Tallarook;
May all the frogs in Doogalook

Sing every night in Tallarook;
May Reedy Creek create a brook
To swamp the flats in Tallarook;
May rabbits ever find a nook
To breed apace in Tallarook;
May Sin Ye Sun and Sam Ah Fook
Steal all the fowls in Tallarook;
May Ikey Moses make a book
To stiffen sport in Tallarook;
May sirens fair as Lalla Rook
Tempt all old men in Tallarook;
May every paddock yield a stook
Of smutty wheat in Tallarook;
May good St Peter overlook
The good deeds done in Tallarook;
May each Don Juan who forsook
His sweetheart live in Tallarook;
May all who Matthew's pledges took
Get rolling drunk in Tallarook;
May every pigeon breed a rook
To spoil the crops in Tallarook;
May I get ague, gout and fluke
If I drink rum in Tallarook.

ANON.

Talking and writing

1 What do you think McQuade has got against the town of Tallarook?

2 Make up a curse against a place you dislike – school, perhaps?

This is probably the commonest type of curse – in which a person hurls insults at another person.

You!

You!
Your head is like a hollow drum.
You!
Your eyes are like balls of flame.
You!
Your ears are like fans for blowing fire.
You!
Your nostril is like a mouse's hole.
You!
Your mouth is like a lump of mud.
You!
Your hands are like drum-sticks.
You!
Your belly is like a pot of bad water.
You!
Your legs are like wooden posts.
You!
Your backside is like a mountain-top.

TRADITIONAL AFRICAN

Writing

Try it yourself. Write your own insults poem.

10: Riddles and Kennings

Riddles

Riddles have been popular since Anglo-Saxon times. This riddle was written over a thousand years ago. Can you solve it?

An Anglo-Saxon Riddle

I'm by nature solitary, scarred by spear
and wounded by sword, weary of battle.
I frequently see the face of war, and fight
hateful enemies; yet I hold no hope
of help being brought to me in the battle,
before I'm eventually done to death.
In the stronghold of the city sharp-edged swords,
skilfully forged in the flame by smiths,
bite deeply into me. I can but await
a more fearsome encounter; it is not for me
to discover in the city any of those doctors
who heal grievous wounds with roots and herbs.
The scars from sword wounds gape wider and wider;
death blows are dealt me by day and by night.

Translated by KEVIN CROSSLEY-HOLLAND

Kennings

A kenning is rather like a short riddle. It consists of a descriptive phrase which is used instead of a noun. Anglo-Saxon poets used many kennings in their poems. For example, the sea is sometimes described as 'the whale-road' or 'the seal-road'.

Here are some other examples of kennings:
world-candle – the sun
battle-adder – an arrow
spear-tree – a warrior
God's bright beacon – the sun.

Can you work out what these kennings refer to:
swan-path?
bone-house?
oar-steed?

Writing

Make up kennings of your own for some of the following: tree, house, moon, stars, lake, mountain, puddle, television, guitar, aeroplane, fountain pen, lawn mower, computer.

Here are some modern riddles:

1

I have no voice and yet I speak to you,
I tell of all things in the world that people do;
I have leaves, but I am not a tree,
I have pages, but I am not a bride or royalty;
I have a spine and hinges, but I am not a man or a door,
I have told you all...I cannot tell you more.

JOHN CUNLIFFE

2

In rainy squall or pattering shower,
I open like a sudden flower;
But when the wind blows strong to gale,
I huddle close and furl my sail;
Then, peg-leg hopping down the street,
I follow close my master's feet.

JOHN CUNLIFFE

3

A many-tongued monster roared over the hill,
That never, oh never, could eat its fill;
Both houses and trees, it devoured them all,
Then covered the scene with a tattered pall.

JOHN CUNLIFFE

4
Falls

This fall enfolds the drowsy land;
This drops fool or prince in fortune's hand;
This brings the sailor safe from the sea;
This brings wealth where none before could be.

(*There is a separate answer for each line in 4.*)

JOHN CUNLIFFE

5

Two fathers and two sons
Went fishing from the beach
Altogether caught three fishes
And that was one fish each.
Does that sound rather odd to you?
Well, try it through again,
And when you think you've worked it out –
Explain.

ERIC FINNEY

Writing

1 Choose an object and make up a riddle about it.
   To help you get some ideas for your riddle, ask yourself these questions: What does the object look like? What is it used for? What would it feel like to be that object?

The easiest way to write a riddle is to write as though the object is speaking, as John Cunliffe does in riddles 1 and 2. If you cannot think of a way to start, begin with a statement such as 'I am...', 'I have...' or 'My...'.

2 Look again at riddle 4. This is a clever riddle, because it is four riddles in one, the answers being linked by the fact that each of the four words ends in – fall.

Make a list of words that begin with either back- or head-. Try to make up your own four-line riddle about different kinds of backs or heads.

11: Wish Poems

Secret Wishes on a Bad Day

While I wait for the bus
  I secretly wish
that Miss wouldn't shout at us.

When I arrive at school
  I secretly wish
Peter wasn't such a fool.

When Sara tells him off
  I secretly wish
she was a member of staff.

When someone picks on me
  I secretly wish
there was another me.

When we go out to games
  I secretly wish
I could be at home with James.

When we sit where we like
  I secretly wish
that I was the most well-liked.

While we have lunch in hall
  I secretly wish
I was grown up and tall.

When the afternoon comes
  I secretly wish
Sema would do all my sums.

When asked to read at two
  I secretly wish
I really didn't have to.

When I don't want to be taught
  I secretly wish
that I won't get caught.

When we go to the baths
  I secretly wish
the boys didn't push you in for laughs.

When Rob pulls my wet hair
  I secretly wish
boys weren't allowed in there.

Before it's time to go home
  I secretly wish
Julie and I were alone.

On my way down the lane
  I secretly wish
I had another name –

Miss has called it out all day
    I secretly wish
I could run far far away.

As I wait for the bus
    I secretly wish
adults went to school not us.

DIANE BROOKENS

Talking and writing

1 When we have a bad day and things go wrong for us, it is natural for us to wish things were different. In pairs, talk about all the things the girl in the poem wishes were different.

2 In pairs, talk about any bad days you have had recently, perhaps because you got soaked on the way to school, you forgot to do something, you were picked on for some reason or because you were feeling ill or you had an accident and hurt yourself.

3 Imagine you had a dreadful day when absolutely everything that could go wrong went wrong – from the moment you woke up late, until when you were lying in bed exhausted, unable to get to sleep late that night. With your partner, make a list of all the things that could go wrong on such a dreadful day. Then, write a poem together called 'Secret wishes on a dreadful day.' Here is the first verse from such a poem. Notice that it rhymes, but do not worry if your verses do not rhyme.

When I woke up at a quarter past eight
   I secretly wished
that I could press Pause to make the bus wait...

4 Think about times when something unpleasant is
happening to you and you wish that you were elsewhere and
were doing something completely different. For example,
when you are about to be given an injection at the dentist's,
or when you are about to have a test to which you don't
know the answers, or when an adult is about to question
you about something you have done. Write a poem called 'I
secretly wish'. Either make up your own beginning or start it
like this:
   When I'm lying in the dentist's chair
     waiting to have an injection
   I secretly wish...

5 What are your secret wishes? If you had three wishes, what
would you wish for? Write either a serious poem or a
humorous poem called 'If I had three wishes.'

I wish I were...

When the gong sounds ten in the morning and I
   walk to school by our lane,
Every day I meet the hawker crying, 'Bangles, crystal
   bangles!'
There is nothing to hurry him on, there is no road he
   must take, no place he must go to, no time when he
   must come home.
I wish I were a hawker, spending my day in the road,
   crying, 'Bangles, crystal bangles!'

When at four in the afternoon I come back from the
    school,
I can see through the gate of that house the gardener
    digging the ground.
He does what he likes with his spade, he soils his clothes
    with dust,
Nobody takes him to task if he gets baked in the sun or
    gets wet.
I wish I were a gardener digging away at the garden
    with nobody to stop me from digging.

Just as it gets dark in the evening and my mother sends
    me to bed,
I can see through my open window the watchman
    walking up and down.
The lane is dark and lonely, and the street-lamp stands
Like a giant with one red eye in its head.
The watchman swings his lantern and walks with his
    shadow at his side, and never once goes to bed in his
    life.
I wish I were a watchman walking the streets all night,
    chasing the shadows with my lantern.

RABINDRANATH TAGORE

Talking and writing

1 Talk about why the boy in the poem wishes he were (a) a hawker, (b) a gardener, (c) a watchman. What is it that he thinks is attractive about the lives they lead compared to the life he leads?

2 Think about people you know or come into contact with; for example the people you see on your way to and from school, or when you go into your local town. Which of their lifestyles appeal to you far more than your own? Talk about why, then write a poem 'I wish I were...'

Here is a poem about a different kind of wishing. D.H. Lawrence wishes that people would not behave in a particular way.

Talk

I wish people, when you sit near them,
wouldn't think it necessary to make conversation
and send thin draughts of words
blowing down your neck and your ears
and giving you a cold in your inside.

D.H. LAWRENCE

Talking and writing

1 What does D.H. Lawrence wish people would not do?

2 Which words and phrases does he use to convey how much he dislikes such behaviour?

3 We all find certain things irritating or annoying. Think of the things people say or do, and the habits that they have, which you find annoying. For example, the way an elderly relative always comments on your appearance, the way smokers drop ash everywhere, or the way your parents won't allow you to do something you want to do.

Write your own poem about something you wish people would not do. Either use one of the beginnings below or make up your own beginning:

I wish that people...
I wish that grown-ups...
I wish that teachers...

What Would You Like to be When You Grow Up, Little Girl?

I'd like to be a model girl, lithe and long and lean;
I'd like to be a TV star, shining from the screen:

I'd like to be an actress, and strut upon the stage;
I'd like to be a poet, printed on this page:

I'd like to be a busy nurse, smoothing down the sheets;
I'd like to be an usherette, and show you to your seats:

I'd like to be a banker, and make a lot of money;
I'd like to be a bee-keeper, and bask on bread and honey:

I'd like to be a dancer, and dance the disco beat;
I'd like to be a traffic warden, storming down the street:

I'd like to be a hairdresser, with blower, brush and comb;
I'd like to be a Romany, the whole wide world to roam:

I'd like to be an air hostess, and soar across the seas;
I'd like to be a doctor, and dose you when you sneeze:

I'd like to be in parliament, and speak a speech for you;
I'd like to be a High Court Judge, and try a case or two:

I'd like to be a teacher, and quell you with one look;
I'd like to be an artist, and illustrate this book:

I'd like to be a gymnast, and balance on a bar;
I'd like to be a grand chauffeur, and drive a dashing car:

I'd like to be a skater, racing round a rink;
I'd like to be just *anything*...I think!

JENNY CRAIG

Writing

1 What career would you like to have when you are grown up, if you could have your wish come true? Make a list of all the reasons why you would like to have that career and all the things you would enjoy doing. Using these ideas, write your own 'I'd like to be' poem.

2 When you daydream, you can imagine yourself having all kinds of adventures. For example, you can imagine you are a princess or a medieval knight, a pirate or a smuggler, a time-traveller or a superhero, an inventor or a record-breaker. Or you can imagine yourself as your favourite TV or comic character or that you are a dragon or a robot. If your daydream came true, who would you like to be? Think of all the things that could happen if your daydream came true and use the ideas to write a poem beginning 'I'd like to be...'

3 If you could change yourself into any object you wished, what would you become? A camera? A pen? A mirror? A motor bike? A space ship?

Choose any object you wish, think about what it would be like to be that object and the things you could do, if you were. Then write a poem about the object beginning 'I'd like to be...'. Here are the first two lines of such a poem:

I'd like to be a mirror, watching from the wall,
Capturing everybody, reflecting on them all...

12: Epitaphs

An epitaph is an inscription on a tombstone. Sometimes, a verse is carved on the tombstone. Here are some unusual ones:

JOHN HYDE,
Dyer

Here lies JOHN HYDE;
He first liv'd, and then he died;
He dyed to live, and lived to dye,
And hopes to live eternally.

Here Lies JOE BROWN, Tailor,
Cut off in the Prime of Life.

ARCHBISHOP POTTER

Alack, alack and well-a-day;
Potter himself is turned to clay.

A MUSIC TEACHER

Stephen and time
Are now both even:
Stephen beat time
Now time's beat Stephen.

HERE
LIES
LESTER MOORE
FOUR SLUGS
FROM A44
NO LES
NO MORE

MARY WEARY,
Housewife

Dere friends I am going
Where washing ain't done
Or cooking or sewing;
Don't mourn for me now
Or weep for me never:
For I go to do nothing
Forever and ever.

Poor MARTHA SNELL
   Her's gone away
Her would if her could
   But her couldn't stay;
Her had two swoln legs
   And a baddish cough
But her legs it was
   As carried her off

JONATHAN POUND

Here lies the body of Jonathan Pound,
Who was lost at sea and never found.

EMMA AND MARIA LITTLEBOY

Two littleboys lie here.
Yet strange to say
The littleboys
Are girls.

Here lies JOHN SMITH, exactly eight,
Who was given a handsome chemistry set.
Here also lies his sister, Maria.
Or what was left of them after the fire.

Here lies a family dog called ROVER:
His pampered life at last is over.
On Rover more than on each other
Love was bestowed by Dad and Mother.

ROY FULLER

Writing

Study these epitaphs, then write some yourself. Here are some suggestions of people you could write epitaphs for:

1 A teacher such as a maths teacher, a science teacher, a PE teacher, an English teacher, a headteacher. . . .

2 A tradesperson such a butcher, a baker, a car mechanic, a cook, a carpenter. . . .

3 A pet – a dog, a cat, a hamster, a budgie, a gerbil, a goldfish. . . .

4 A person with an unusual name such as Hotpot, Greasepaint, Coalface, Truebody. . . .

5 A sister and her brother who met their fate in an unusual way, as John Smith and Maria did. . . .

6 A member of a pop group with a bizarre name, for example: The Slugs, Elastic Hairnet, Telephone Message, Grasshopper Pie. . . .

13: Letter Poems and Alphabet Poems

Letter Poems

Letter poems can be divided into two types – those about the shapes of letters and those about the sounds of letters. Stanley Cook's poem about the letter *H* belongs to the first type, focussing on the shape of the letter and what it suggests. Rony Robinson's *Alf Abets* is a word-play poem in which the writer develops a nonsense rhyme based on the sounds of the letters of the alphabet.

H

H goes to make the throne
A great man sits on
Dangling his legs in the air
Like a baby from a high chair.

STANLEY COOK

Alf Abets

Eighteen apples
Be like me
See if you can
Deep blue sea.
Easy does it
Every time
Jeannie likes me
Ain't you mine.
I eyed Ivor
Jays can fly
Kay's a singer
Elephants cry.
Emma's empty
Anyway
Owners only
Peas, please pay.
Queue less quickly
Aren't you nice
Especially Sarah
Teach her twice.
You'll know better
VIPs
What a whopper
Ex-wife sees.

Ain't you coming
Beans for tea
Seems quite pleasant
Dean can't see.
Emus rattle
If they die
Jeans are shrinking
Hate your tie.
I'm an eyeful
Jacob's knot
Cake's for eating
Elton's hot.
Empty bottles
Any time
Opening over
Peace in our time.
Cumin powder
Artist's nose
Esther argues
Tease her toes.
Universal
Veal ham pie
Double youth club
Extra wise.

RONY ROBINSON

Talking and writing

1 Stanley Cook's poem is a simple comparison poem. Do you think the comparison he makes is an appropriate one? Why?

What else is a capital H like?

2 Choose another capital letter and write a poem in which you make a comparison which is suggested by the letter's shape.

In groups

1 In groups of four, prepare a reading of Rony Robinson's poem *Alf Abets*. First, go through the poem deciding which lines each of you are going to read. Then, experiment with different ways of saying the lines. Remember that the poem is meant to be fun, so try to think up as many ways as possible of presenting it in an amusing way.

After all the groups have presented their readings, discuss whose reading was the most successful and decide why.

2 In your groups, write your own word-play poems on the sounds of the letters of the alphabet. Try to include some rhymes, but don't worry if you cannot manage to make it rhyme. Here's how one group started their Alf Abets poem:

Ate nine canaries
Before I had a swim
Seen one, seen them all
Decidedly dim...

When you have written your group poem, prepare a reading of it and present it to the other groups.

Alphabet Poems

The most common type of alphabet poem is a poem of
twenty-six lines, each line beginning with a different letter of
the alphabet, as in the poem *Animal Alphabet*. Another type
of alphabet poem is one which has only twenty-six words,
the first word starting with the letter A, the next with the
letter B and so on through the alphabet. Wes Magee's *An
A-Z of Pop Groups* is an example of this type of alphabet
poem.

Animal Alphabet

Alligator, beetle, porcupine, whale,
Bobolink, panther, dragonfly, snail,
Crocodile, monkey, buffalo, hare,
Dromedary, leopard, mud turtle, bear,
Elephant, badger, pelican, ox,
Flying fish, reindeer, anaconda, fox,
Guinea pig, dolphin, antelope, goose,
Hummingbird, weasel, pickerel, moose,
Ibex, rhinoceros, owl, kangaroo,
Jackal, opossum, toad, cockatoo,
Kingfisher, peacock, anteater, bat,
Lizard, ichneumon, honeybee, rat,
Mockingbird, camel, grasshopper, mouse,
Nightingale, spider, cuttlefish, grouse,
Ocelot, pheasant, wolverine, auk,
Periwinkle, ermine, katydid, hawk,
Quail, hippopotamus, armadillo, moth,
Rattlesnake, lion, woodpecker, sloth,
Salamander, goldfinch, angleworm, dog,

Tiger, flamingo, scorpion, frog,
Unicorn, ostrich, nautilus, mole,
Viper, gorilla, basilisk, sole,
Whippoorwill, beaver, centipede, fawn,
Xema, canary, tadpole, swan,
Yellowhammer, eagle, hyena, lark,
Zebra, chameleon, butterfly, shark.

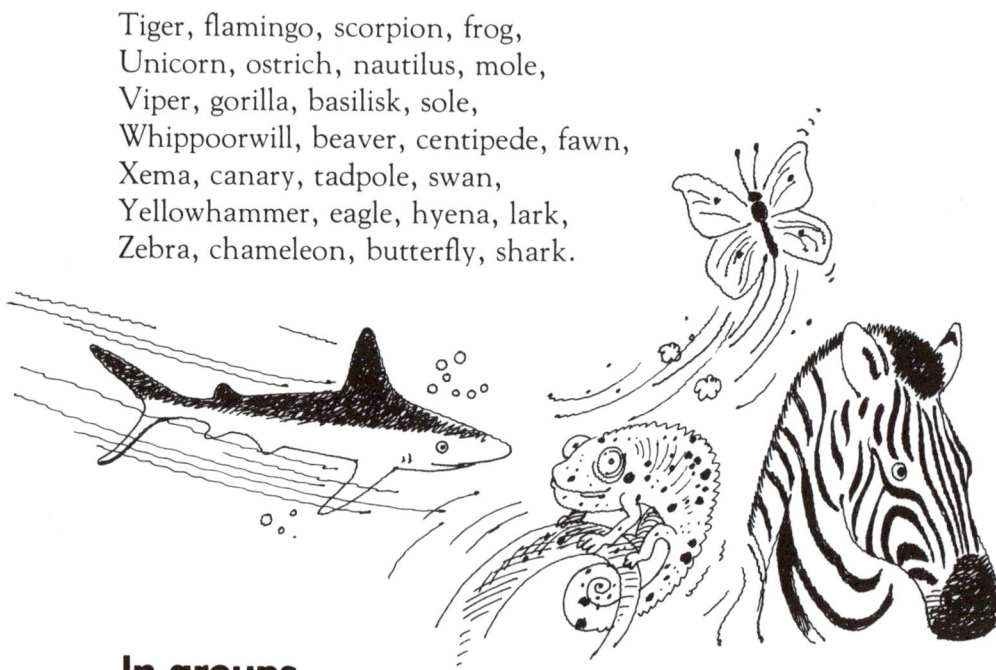

In groups

The verse 'Alligator, beetle, porcupine, whale' contains the names of 104 animals, birds, fish and insects! Work in a group and try to produce a similar poem on a different subject, e.g. A plant alphabet, listing the names of trees, flowers and vegetables; a place-names alphabet; an alphabet of first names; or an alphabet of everyday things.

First, make a list of words letter by letter. Then, try to find 13 pairs of rhyming words that you might be able to use to end the lines of your poem. Before you start to fit the poem together, look again at *Animal Alphabet*. Notice how the verse has a strong rhythm because each line has nine syllables and the verse is arranged in pairs of lines which rhyme. As you write, see if you can make your poem fit this pattern.

An A-Z of Pop Groups

Arm Band
Creeping Daughters
Egg Flops
Giant Heart
International Jets
Kissing Llama
Mutant Noise
Oblong Peanut

Queer Rabbit
Silver Tongues
Ugly Vicar
Wet Xmas
Yellow Zebra

WES MAGEE

Writing

1 Write your own A-Z poem. Do not necessarily restrict
yourself to writing only twenty-six words. For example, your
own A-Z of Pop Groups might begin:
    Angie's Avenging Angels
    Boneshaker and the Bluebottles...
Here are some other suggestions for A-Z poems:
    An A-Z of Horror Movies
    An A-Z of Space Beasts
    An A-Z of Circus Acts
    An A-Z of Superstars

2 Write an A-Z of adjectives. Here's how one girl started
such a poem:
    A is anxious, afraid and alarming.
    B is beautiful, bossy and busy.
    C is confident, cunning and charming...

14: Chants and Songs

The School Ghoul

Ghoul, ghoul, I am the ghoul,
I hide by the dustbins just outside your school.
Ghoul, ghoul, I am the ghoul.

Ghoul, ghoul, I am the ghoul,
I live on the banks of a dark, slimy pool.
Ghoul, ghoul, I am the ghoul.

Ghoul, ghoul, I am the ghoul,
I'm nasty and dirty and vicious and cruel.
Ghoul, ghoul, I am the ghoul.

Ghoul, ghoul, I am the ghoul,
I bite like a tiger and kick like a mule.
Ghoul, ghoul, I am the ghoul.

Ghoul, ghoul, I am the ghoul,
I'll get you and eat you if you play the fool.
Ghoul, ghoul, I am the ghoul.

Ghoul, ghoul, I am the ghoul,
There'll be nothing left except blood in a pool.
Ghoul, ghoul, I am the ghoul.

IAN LARMONT

Group work

1 Work in groups of three and prepare a presentation of the poem. Go through the poem and decide which of you is going to speak each line. For example, are you each going to take it in turns to say a whole verse or are all three of you going to chant the lines 'Ghoul, ghoul, I am the ghoul'? Can you think of movements, music or sounds that would make your presentation more dramatic? Experiment with different ways of speaking and presenting the poem, then learn it and present it to the other groups. Finally, discuss which ways of presenting the poem were most effective and why.

2 In your groups, write a similar poem. It could be the chant of an ogre or a troll, a spectre or a spook, a gremlin or a goblin, a dragon or a kraken, a giant or a genie. Don't worry if you cannot make it rhyme. Here is the start of a similar chant, *The Spectre's Song*:

Spectre, spectre, I am the spectre,
I'm the spectre who lurks under the stairs
Spectre, spectre, I am the spectre...

The Song of Tyrannosaurus Rex

I'm a rock, I'm a mountain, I'm a hammer and a nail
I'm an army and a navy, I'm a force ten gale

I'm a trooper, I'm a tearaway, and time will never see
Another king, or anything, that fights like me

I'm a sinner, I'm a winner, I'm a one-man government
I'm the will of the people, I'm the force that's never spent

I'm a business and a factory, the work-force and the boss
I'm the brains and the belly and I never make a loss

I'm a monumental mason and the gravestones that I make
Are carved of flesh and bone from the carcases I take

I'm a god, I'm a ghost, I'm the creak on the stairs
I'm the grin that listens in when people say their prayers

I'm a crane, I'm a lorry, I'm a brand-new motorway
I set like concrete and I'm here to stay

O I'm big and I'm bad and I'm bold and I'm free
And the world will never see another villain like me

For I swagger and I swallow and the earth is my hotel
And I chew my meat in heaven and I lash my tail in hell!

WILLIAM SCAMMELL

Talking and writing

1 Talk about how William Scammell uses comparisons in the poem to convey what an awesome monster Tyrannosaurus Rex is.
Pick out the comparisons he uses to say
(a) how strong Tyrannosaurus Rex is;
(b) how huge Tyrannosaurus Rex is;
(c) how tough Tyrannosaurus Rex is;
(d) how fierce Tyrannosaurus Rex is;
(e) how vicious Tyrannosaurus Rex is;
(f) how powerful Tyrannosaurus Rex is.

Which two lines do you think are the most effective in putting across the idea that Tyrannosaurus Rex is a brutal, fearless monster?

2 The poem has a very strong rhythm, which adds to its effect. It helps to stress Tyrannosaurus Rex's strength and power. In groups of three, prepare a reading of the poem, in which you make use of the rhythm to help to convey the ideas expressed in the poem.

3 In his poem, William Scammell does not make the Tyrannosaurus Rex boast about its particular features, such as its teeth, each as long as the blade of a dagger, which it used to slice and tear flesh. Below are some pictures of other dinosaurs. Study them closely and talk about their particular features, e.g. the spikes on the back of stegosaurus. Choose one of them and think of words you could use and comparisons you could make in order to describe each of its features – its head, its mouth, its teeth, its body, its feet, its claws, etc. Then, write your own poem: The song of the dinosaur.

Here is another song with a strong rhythm:

Sewing Machine

I'm faster, I'm faster than fingers,
            much faster.
No mistress can match me, no mistress
            nor master.
My bobbin is racing to feed in the
            thread,
Pink, purple, grey, green, lemon-yellow
            or red.
My needle, my needle, my slim, sharp
            steel needle.
Makes tiny, neat stitches in trousers
            and dresses
And firmly my silver foot presses,
            it presses.
I'm faster, I'm faster than fingers,
            much faster.

GWEN DUNN

Talking and writing

1 Work with a partner and take it in turns to read the poem aloud. Notice how the rhythm of the poem manages to capture the rhythm of a sewing machine at work.

2 Try to write a poem about a machine of some kind in which you make use of rhythm to convey the machine's movement.

For example, you might write about a train or a fairground machine, a washing-machine or a typewriter, a combine-harvester or a pneumatic drill. Here is the start of such a poem about a typewriter:

The song of the typewriter
I pitter and I patter
As I tap across the page...

The Snake Song

Neither legs nor arms have I
But I crawl on my belly
And I have
Venom, venom, venom!

Neither horns nor hoofs have I
But I spit with my tongue
And I have
Venom, venom, venom!

Neither bows nor guns have I
But I flash fast my tongue
And I have
Venom, venom, venom!

Neither radar nor missiles have I
But I stare with my eyes
And I have
Venom, venom, venom!

I master every movement
For I jump, run and swim
And I spit
Venom, venom, venom!

JOHN MBITI

Talking and writing

1 What impression does the song give of the snake? Talk
about how John Mbiti creates this impression.

Discuss the pattern of the first four verses. How and why is
the fifth verse different from the first four verses?

Which verse did you find most effective? Explain why.

2 Try it yourself. Write the song of another dangerous
animal such as a crocodile, an alligator, a shark, a tiger, a
wolf, a vulture, a tarantula or a piranha fish. You could, if
you wish, use exactly the same verse pattern as John Mbiti
has used. Here is an example of the first verse from such a
poem:

The song of the scorpion
Neither motor nor engine have I
But I scuttle over the sand
And I can
Sting, sting, sting!